FULL SCORE
WSB-10-006

吹奏楽譜 ブラスロック・シリーズ

BRASS ROCK

威風堂々 Brass Rock

作曲：Edward Elgar　編曲：郷間幹男

楽器編成表

Piccolo	B♭ Trumpet 1	Drums
Flutes 1（& *2）	B♭ Trumpet 2	Conga
*Oboe	*B♭ Trumpet 3	Percussion 1
*Bassoon	F Horns 1（& *2）	…Tambourine, Cowbell
*E♭ Clarinet	F Horns 3（& *4）	Percussion 2
B♭ Clarinet 1	Trombone 1	…Wind Chime, Triangle, Sus.Cymbal
B♭ Clarinet 2	Trombone 2	
*B♭ Clarinet 3	*Trombone 3	Glockenspiel
*Alto Clarinet	Euphonium	
Bass Clarinet	Tuba	Full Score
Alto Saxophone 1	Electric Bass (String Bass)	
*Alto Saxophone 2		
Tenor Saxophone		
Baritone Saxophone		

＊イタリック表記の楽譜はオプション

ご注文について

ウィンズスコアの商品は全国の楽器店、ならびに書店にてお求めになれますが、店頭でのご購入が困難な場合、当社PC&モバイルサイト・FAX・電話からのご注文で、直接ご購入が可能です。

◎当社PCサイトでのご注文方法

http://www.winds-score.com

上記のURLへアクセスし、WEBショップにてご注文ください。

◎FAXでのご注文方法

FAX.03-6809-0594

24時間、ご注文を承ります。当社サイトよりFAXご注文用紙をダウンロードし、印刷、ご記入の上ご送信ください。

◎お電話でのご注文方法

TEL.0120-713-771

営業時間内に電話いただければ、電話にてご注文を承ります。

◎モバイルサイトでのご注文方法

右のQRコードを読み取ってアクセスいただくか、URLを直接ご入力ください。

※この出版物の全部または一部を権利者に無断で複製(コピー)することは、著作権の侵害にあたり、著作権法により罰せられます。

※造本には十分注意しておりますが、万一、落丁・乱丁などの不良品がありましたらお取り替えいたします。また、ご意見・ご感想もホームページより受け付けておりますので、お気軽にお問い合わせください。

Piccolo

威風堂々 Brass Rock

Comp.by Edward William Elgar
Arr. by Mikio Gohma

Oboe

威風堂々 Brass Rock

Comp.by Edward William Elgar
Arr. by Mikio Gohma

E♭ Clarinet

威風堂々 Brass Rock

Comp.by Edward William Elgar
Arr. by Mikio Gohma

B♭ Clarinet 2

威風堂々 Brass Rock

Comp.by Edward William Elgar
Arr. by Mikio Gohma

Alto Saxophone 1

威風堂々 Brass Rock

Tenor Saxophone

威風堂々 Brass Rock

Comp.by Edward William Elgar
Arr. by Mikio Gohma

威風堂々 Brass Rock

B♭ Trumpet 1

Comp.by Edward William Elgar
Arr. by Mikio Gohma

B♭ Trumpet 2

威風堂々 Brass Rock

Comp. by Edward William Elgar
Arr. by Mikio Gohma

B♭ Trumpet 3

威風堂々 Brass Rock

Trombone 3

威風堂々 Brass Rock

Comp.by Edward William Elgar
Arr. by Mikio Gohma

威風堂々 Brass Rock

Euphonium

Comp.by Edward William Elgar
Arr. by Mikio Gohma

Electric Bass Guitar
(String Bass)

威風堂々 Brass Rock

Comp.by Edward William Elgar
Arr. by Mikio Gohma

Conga

威風堂々 Brass Rock

Comp.by Edward William Elgar
Arr. by Mikio Gohma

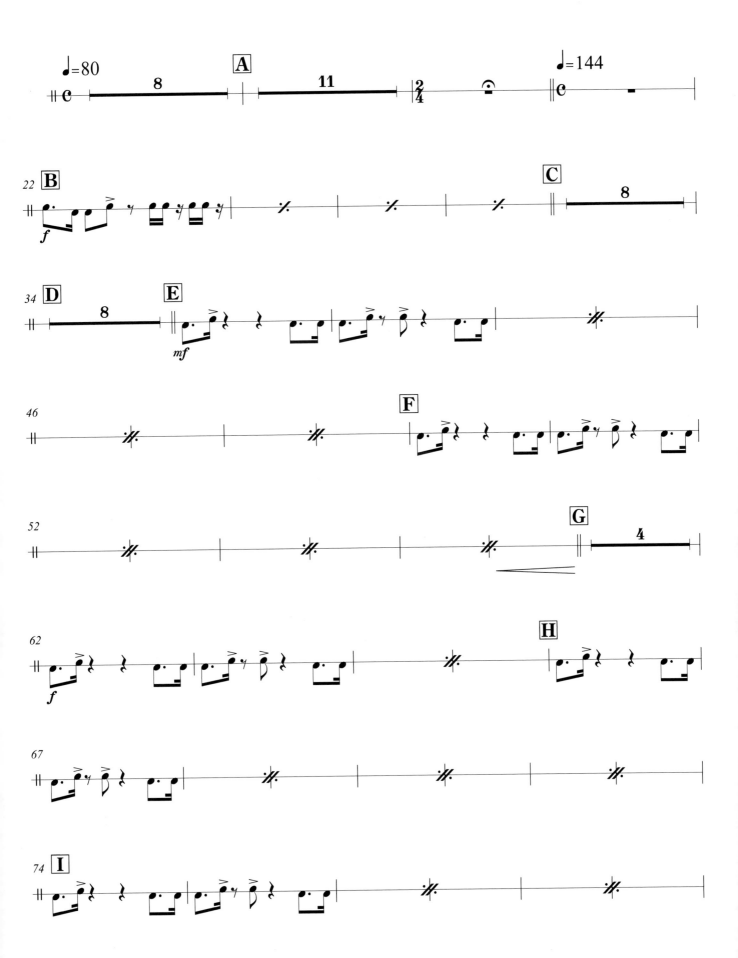

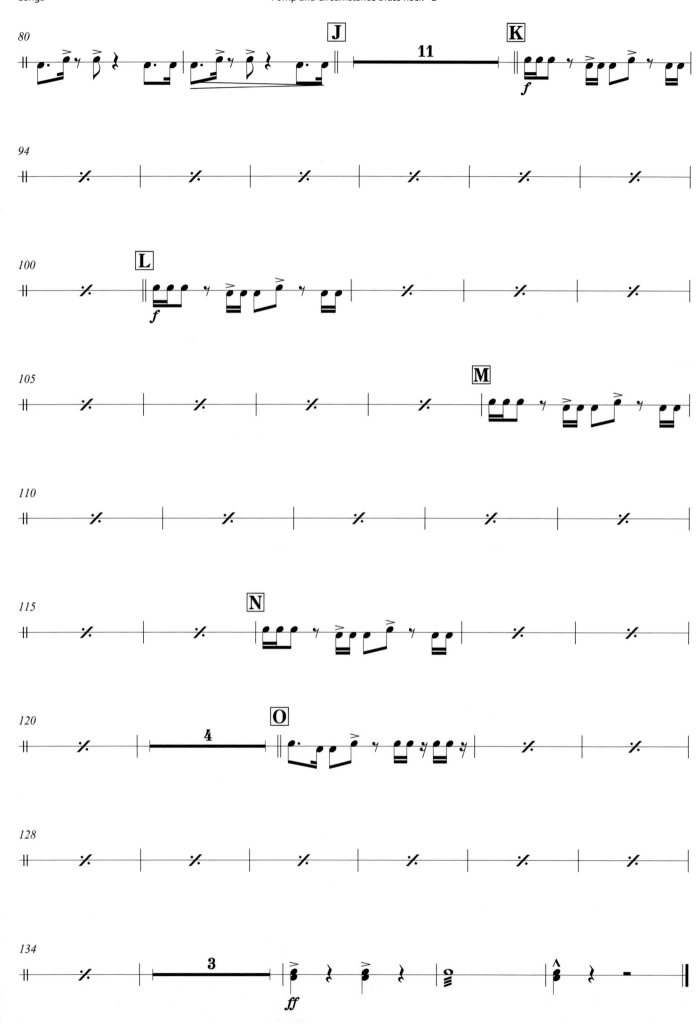

Percussion 1
(Tambourine, Cowbell)

威風堂々 Brass Rock

Comp.by Edward William Elgar
Arr. by Mikio Gohma

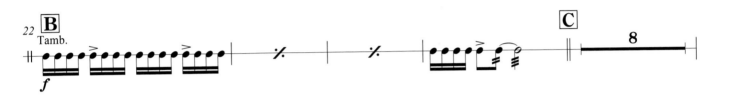
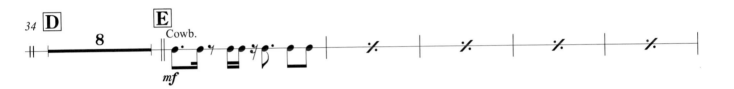

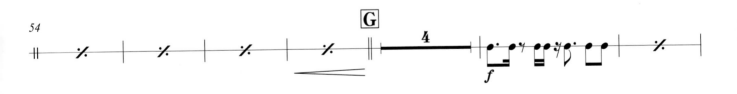
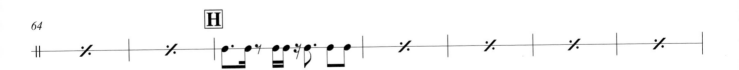

Percussion 1
(Tambourine, Cowbell)

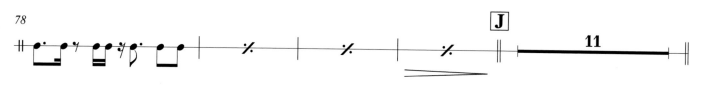

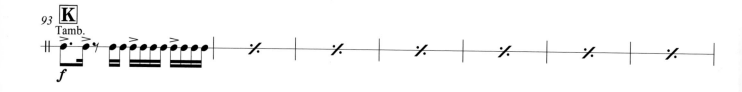

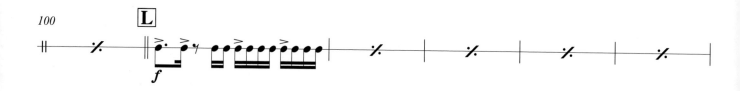

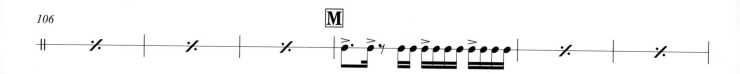

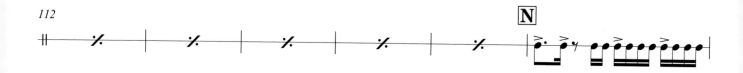

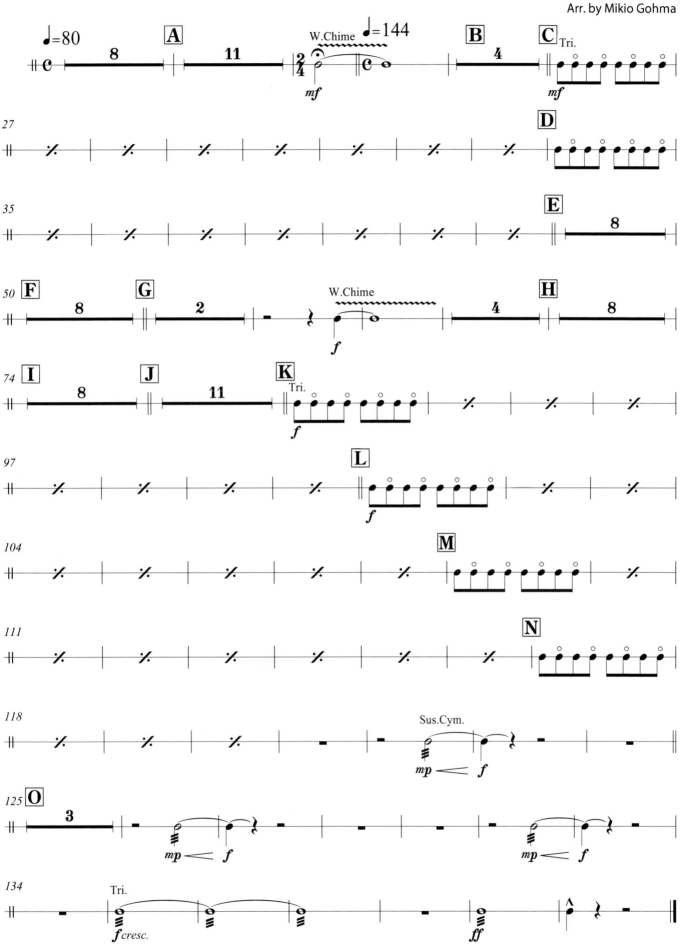